TEMPERATE FORESTS

John Woodward

 www.heinemannraintree.com
Visit our website to find out more information about Heinemann-Raintree books.

To order:
☎ Phone 888-454-2279
💻 Visit www.heinemannraintree.com to browse our catalog and order online.

Published in 2011 by Heinemann-Raintree books, an imprint of Capstone Global Library, LLC, Chicago, Illinois

© 2011 The Brown Reference Group Ltd.

For The Brown Reference Group Ltd:
Editorial Director: Lindsey Lowe
Managing Editor: Tim Harris
Editor: Jolyon Goddard
Original consultant: Dr. Mark Hostetler,
Department of Wildlife Ecology and Conservation, University of Florida
Designers: Reg Cox, Joan Curtis
Picture researcher: Clare Newman
Production Director: Alastair Gourlay

Printed in the USA

ISBN: 978-1-432-94180-2; 978-1-432-94184-0 (set)
14 13 12 11 10
10 9 8 7 6 5 4 3 2 1

Library of Congress Cataloging-in-Publication Data

Woodward, John, 1954-
  Temperate forests / John Woodward.
    p. cm.—(Biomes atlases)
  Includes bibliographical references and index.
  ISBN 978-1-4329-4180-2 (hc)
  1. Forest ecology—Juvenile literature. 2. Forest ecology—Maps for children. I. Title.
  QH541.5.F6W68 2011
  577.3—dc22   2010013029

Every effort has been made to contact copyright holders of any material reproduced in this book. Any omissions will be rectified in subsequent printings if notice is given to the publisher.

All the Internet addresses (URLs) given in this book were valid at the time of going to press. However, due to the dynamic nature of the Internet, some addresses may have changed, or sites may have changed or ceased to exist since publication. While the author and publisher regret any inconvenience this may cause readers, no responsibility for any such changes can be accepted by either the author or the publisher.

About this Book

The introductory pages of this book describe the world's biomes and then the temperate forest biome. The five main chapters look at different aspects of temperate forests: climate, plants, animals, people, and the future. Between the chapters are detailed maps that focus on key forest areas. The map pages are shown in the contents in italics, *like this*. Exclamation-point icons on the map pages draw attention to regions where the biome or its wildlife is under threat. Throughout the book you'll also find boxed stories or fact files about temperate forests. The icons here show what the boxes are about. Words in **bold** throughout the book are explained in the glossary at the end of the book. After the glossary is a list of books and websites for further research and an index, allowing you to locate subjects anywhere in the book.

 Climate

 People

 Plants

 Future

 Animals

 Facts

 Extinction

 Under Threat

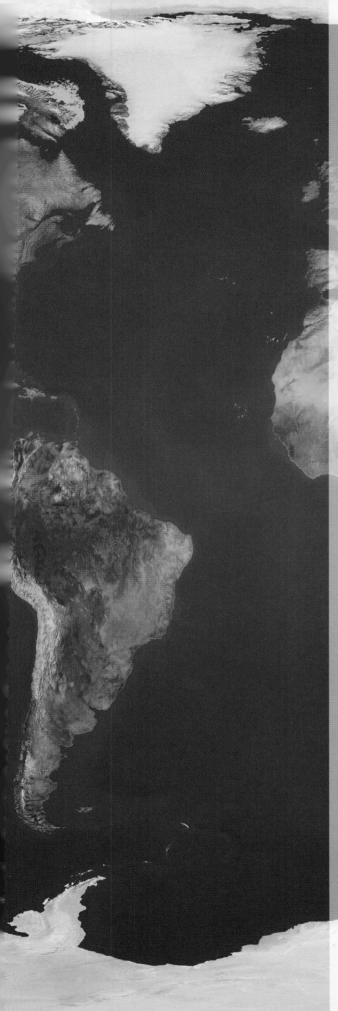

Contents

BIOMES OF THE WORLD

Biologists divide the living world into major zones named biomes. Each biome has its own distinctive climate, plants, and animals.

If you were to walk all the way from the north of Canada to the Amazon **rain forest**, you'd notice the wilderness changing dramatically along the way (see route marked on map to right).

Northern Canada is a freezing and barren place without trees, where only tiny brownish-green plants can survive in the icy ground. But trudge south for long enough and you enter a magical world of **conifer** forests, where moose, caribou, and wolves live. After several weeks, the conifers disappear, and you reach the grass-covered **prairies** of the central United States. The farther south you go, the drier the land gets and the hotter the sunshine feels, until you find yourself hiking through a cactus-filled **desert**. But once you reach southern Mexico, the cacti start to disappear, and strange **tropical** trees begin to take their place. Here, the muggy air is filled with the calls of exotic birds and the drone of tropical insects. Finally, in Colombia you cross the Andes mountain range—whose chilly peaks remind you a little of your starting point—and descend into the dense, swampy jungles of the Amazon rain forest.

Desert is the driest biome. There are hot deserts and cold ones.

Taiga is made up of conifer trees that can survive freezing winters.

Scientists have a special name for the different regions—such as desert, tropical rain forest, and prairie—that you'd pass through on such a journey. They call them **biomes**. Everywhere on Earth can be classified as being in one biome or another, and the same biome often appears in lots of

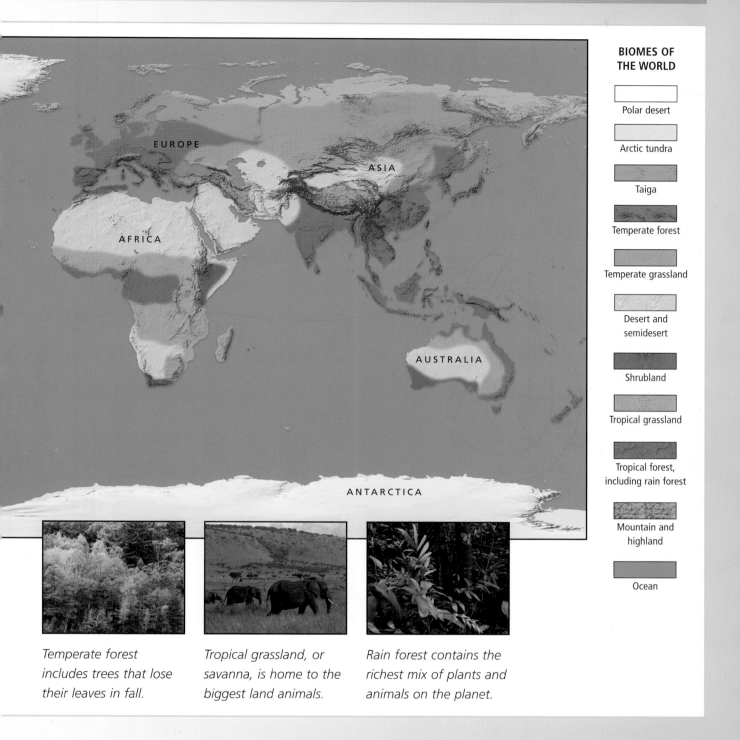

**BIOMES OF
THE WORLD**

Polar desert

Arctic tundra

Taiga

Temperate forest

Temperate grassland

Desert and
semidesert

Shrubland

Tropical grassland

Tropical forest,
including rain forest

Mountain and
highland

Ocean

EUROPE

ASIA

AFRICA

AUSTRALIA

ANTARCTICA

*Temperate forest
includes trees that lose
their leaves in fall.*

*Tropical grassland, or
savanna, is home to the
biggest land animals.*

*Rain forest contains the
richest mix of plants and
animals on the planet.*

different places. For instance, there are areas of rain forest as far apart as Brazil, Africa, and Southeast Asia. Although the plants and animals that inhabit these forests are different, they live in similar ways. Likewise, the prairies of North America are part of the grassland biome, which also occurs in China, Australia, and Argentina. Wherever there are grasslands, there are grazing animals that feed on the grass, as well as large carnivores that hunt and kill the grazers.

The map on this page shows how the world's major biomes fit together to make up the biosphere—the zone of life on Earth.

TEMPERATE FORESTS OF THE WORLD

Every year, the forests of eastern North America blaze with color as the leaves begin to die. The spectacular display is a sign that life in the forest is dominated by the seasons.

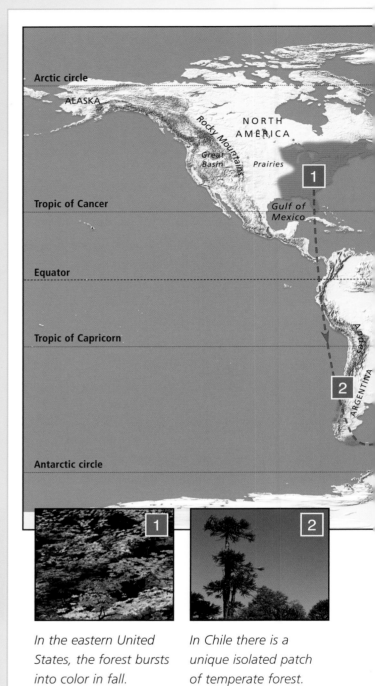

In the eastern United States, the forest bursts into color in fall.

In Chile there is a unique isolated patch of temperate forest.

In the eastern United States, forests are lush and teem with life in spring and summer, but as the months pass, the days get shorter and colder. Starved of energy and water, the plants stop growing. Eventually, most of the soft-stemmed plants seem to die away, while many trees lose their leaves and become bare skeletons. With nothing to eat, most of the animals leave or go underground. Nothing stirs. Yet the plants are not dead; they are just waiting. Eventually, the days will get longer and warmer, and life will start over.

The parts of the world that have this cycle of the seasons—from warm spring and summer to cool fall and winter and back again—are called temperate. Together, the forests that grow in **temperate** countries make up the world's temperate forest biome. The summers are never as hot there as in the warm and wet tropical forests that flank the Amazon River in South America, where the

Sun shines year round. The winters in temperate regions are never as cold as they are near the poles.

Most temperate forest grows in eastern North America, Europe, and eastern Asia. In these places, winter frost stops most trees from growing all year round, so the

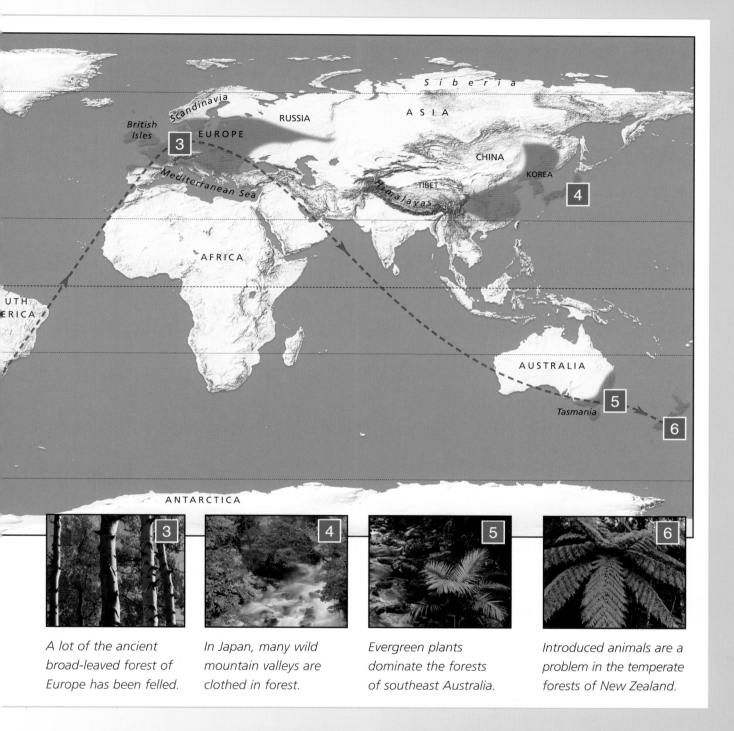

A lot of the ancient broad-leaved forest of Europe has been felled.

In Japan, many wild mountain valleys are clothed in forest.

Evergreen plants dominate the forests of southeast Australia.

Introduced animals are a problem in the temperate forests of New Zealand.

trees shed their leaves and shut down over winter. Such forests are called temperate **deciduous** forests.

In some temperate countries there may be no winter frost. If there is enough rain, the trees keep their leaves and continue growing through winter. The result is temperate **evergreen** rain forest, of the kind that grows in New Zealand and Tasmania. Where there is less rain, there may be long summer droughts, best survived by evergreen trees with leathery leaves. This type of evergreen temperate forest grows in southeast Australia.

EASTERN NORTH AMERICA

Temperate forests once covered the eastern United States and parts of Canada, from the swamps of the deep south to the Great Lakes and beyond into Quebec. Most of these forests are gone, but the surviving ones are world-famous for their glorious leaf color in fall.

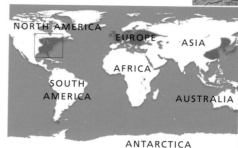

1. Mount Katahdin, Maine
The northern end of the Appalachian Trail. Invasive plants are outcompeting native plants.

2. Adirondack Park
Trails lead visitors through the sugar maples and paper birches. Acid rain is a problem in the park.

Forest Facts

▲ Much of the eastern United States is taken up by the Appalachian Mountains. A broad band of lowlands loops around the south of the mountains from the prairies to the east coast.

▲ The North American temperate forest is rich in animal and plant species. There are more than 27 species of salamanders within the Great Smoky Mountains National Park alone—although many are now affected by a fatal fungal disease that is killing amphibians across the world.

▲ The southern Appalachian Mountains support more than 130 species of trees (the whole of Europe has just 85) and more than 1,500 species of wildflowers.

Left: The fall colors of maple trees are typical of American temperate forest in the north. In the south, though, there is subtropical forest formed by trees that don't lose their leaves in fall.

3. Plymouth, Massachusetts
Pilgrims landed here in 1620 and cleared forests to grow crops.

4. New York City
This is the center of the biggest U.S. urban region, with 17 million people. Air pollution is a problem in the city.

5. Appalachian Mountains
Extend from Newfoundland, Canada, south to Atlanta, Georgia. Flying squirrels are threatened by habitat loss in the mountain forests.

6. Kansas City, Missouri
Here, the original temperate forest faded into dry prairie grassland.

7. Ohio River
When early settlers from Europe crossed the Ohio River they discovered rich farmland. Invasive zebra mussels are outcompeting native mussels in the river.

8. Shenandoah National Park
Created in 1936, this reserve is home to many black bears.

9. Great Smoky Mountains National Park
The warm, flower-strewn forests of the Smoky Mountains are among the world's most beautiful. Introduced wild hogs damage the understory.

10. Delta National Forest, Mississippi
The temperate forest biome extends south to the southern Mississippi flood plain.

The Appalachian Trail

If you think you need a little exercise, you could try hiking most of the length of the American temperate forest biome along the Appalachian Trail. Officially opened in 1937, the trail is the longest footpath in the world. It extends more than 3,360 kilometers (2,100 miles) from Springer Mountain in Georgia to Mount Katahdin in Maine. That's the same as the distance across the Atlantic from South America to Africa. If you manage to hike the whole trail you'll become an expert on temperate forest wildlife—and you'll get to see a whole lot of trees.

TEMPERATE CLIMATES

Earth's temperate forests lie roughly midway between the tropics and the poles. The weather here changes with the seasons. The broad leaves of the trees may turn and fall as winter sets in, but it never gets too dry or too cold for the temperate forest wildlife.

The **temperate climate** is mild—neither extremely hot nor extremely cold. Summers can be hot and dry, but they are rarely so parched that the plants shrivel up or the soil turns to dust. Winters are often cold and snowy, but never as harsh or long-lasting as in the **taiga** forests of Canada, northern Europe, or Siberia. So while the temperate climate is changeable, it is fairly comfortable for much of the year.

The ideal climate for a tree is sunny, warm, and wet, throughout the year, as it is in a tropical rain forest. But for trees outside the steamy equatorial rain forest, the temperate zone is the next best place to be.

Southern Complications

If Earth was a smooth ball, dotted all over with continents and seas, there would be two bands of temperate forest extending around the globe to the north and south of the tropics. The world is not like that, though. Most of the land is concentrated in the north, and the southern **hemisphere** is mostly ocean.

If the African continent extended farther south, the southern tip might have supported temperate forest. As it is, the temperate zone there makes a fine habitat for fish.

South America extends farther south, so you might expect a temperate forest to develop in Argentina, between the tropical zone and the chilly wastes of Antarctica. Instead, most of Argentina is taken up either by dry grassland, called the pampas, or by a cool desert called Patagonia. The reason lies in the west of the continent, where the high Andes mountains form a long barrier between the Argentinian plains and the Pacific Ocean. The wind usually blows from the Pacific in this part of South America, so it has to cross the mountains before it reaches Argentina. As the air rises to pass over the Andes, the moisture it picked up from the ocean cools down and turns to rain, falling on the mountains.

 ## Microclimates

According to world maps of climate, vast areas enjoy exactly the same conditions. It doesn't really work like that, though. A high mountain in the temperate zone can have a virtually arctic climate and arctic-type plants at its peak. Even a steep hill may have a completely different type of climate on each flank, depending on which side faces the Sun. One sheltered valley may be a warm refuge from cold winds, while another may be a frost hollow that regularly fills with heavy, freezing air. These local differences are called microclimates, and they explain why some parts of the temperate forest biome are a patchwork of different trees, while other parts have no trees at all.

In South America, only a small fragment of land, in Chile, has the mild conditions needed by temperate forest. Forests of southern beech trees grow here, and provide a rare and valuable habitat for a unique wildlife.

Gone Forever

Every 100,000 years or so, the world enters the grip of an ice age. The climate gets colder everywhere, and the ice sheets that cover the poles spread out, engulfing vast areas of land and sea. The last ice age ended about 11,000 years ago. At its peak, ice sheets spread well into what are now the United States and northern Europe. The temperate forests were wiped from these regions by the ice, but in North America most of the temperate plant species survived by moving south. In Europe, the plants couldn't move south because the mountain barriers of the Alps and Pyrenees cut off their retreat. Hemmed in by ice to the north and mountains to the south, many European plant species were wiped out altogether—which is why Europe now has fewer species of temperate forest plants than North America.

By the time the moving air reaches the other side of the Andes, it has lost its moisture, so Argentina does not get enough rain to support a forest. Instead, the plains of Argentina are grassland or desert. There is a patch of temperate forest on the western side of the Andes, in Chile, but it is small because it is crammed between the ocean and the barren heights of the mountains.

On the other side of the Pacific, New Zealand and Tasmania have no such problem. Lying in the warm temperate zone, they are swept by oceanic winds that bring plenty of rain—often more than 1 meter (39 inches) each year. The nearby ocean keeps the weather mild all year, with no dry season and no frost. As a result, the islands are clothed in temperate evergreen rain forest.

A few patches of temperate rain forest also grow in southeastern Australia, but only on the oceanic side of the mountain chain, the Great Dividing Range, that extends down the eastern side of the continent. Like the Andes, these mountains catch all the rain swept in

from the ocean on the wind, and the landscape in the temperate zone to the west of the Great Dividing Range is dry grassland. So the area of temperate forest terrain in Australia is only about the same as that of New Zealand, and including Tasmania the total area is smaller than Texas.

The Continental North

The northern hemisphere is totally unlike the southern. Instead of vast expanses of ocean, it has great continental landmasses. In the far north these form an almost continuous ring around the planet, mantled with icy **tundra** and the dark taiga forests of Scandinavia, northern Russia, Siberia, Alaska, and Canada.

South of the taiga lies the temperate zone. Unlike that of the southern hemisphere, the northern temperate zone extends over an immense area of land, covering most of the United States, southern Canada, central and eastern Asia, and Europe. As in the southern hemisphere, however, the terrain and climate make a lot of the area unsuitable for forest.

In western North America, the mountains extending along the Pacific fringe of the continent act as a rain-catching barrier, stripping moisture from the air blowing off the ocean. So the terrain to the east of the mountains is starved of rain. Much of it is desert, extending far north in the **rain shadow** of the Coastal Ranges and the Cascades. This region, known as the Great Basin, is cut off to the east by yet more mountains—the Rockies—so it is also isolated from any moist air from the Gulf of Mexico.

East of the Rockies, desert grades into the dry temperate grasslands of the prairies. Here, as on the Pampas of Argentina, there is not enough rainfall to overcome the drying effects of the wind and sunshine, especially in summer, so forest trees cannot get enough water. A typical temperate forest needs at least 300 millimeters (12 inches) of rain a

New Zealand's climate is not tropical, but some parts receive over twice as much rain as many tropical rain forests. The rain encourages a lush growth of ferns and evergreen trees, forming temperate rain forest.

Temperate forest covers the Great Smoky Mountains National Park in the Appalachian Mountains. Frost destroys the delicate leaves of these trees (inset), so the trees are deciduous—they shed their leaves every year. As fall wears on, the leaves turn red and golden before falling to the ground.

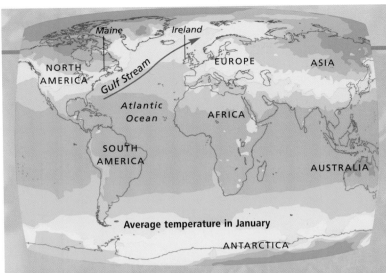

The Gulf Stream carries warm water across the ocean to western Europe. This gives Europe a mild climate, shown orange on this map, while North America and Asia remain cold and blue.

Average temperature in January

Hot Flash

Maine is very cold in winter. Yet across the Atlantic Ocean, western Ireland is farther north, and it hardly ever snows. Why?

An ocean current called the Gulf Stream carries warm water northeast from Florida to Europe. As it swirls around the west coasts of Europe, it warms the air and gives European countries a far milder climate than might be expected. This is why the temperate forest zone in Europe is so much farther north than the same zone in America. Some climatologists fear that global warming may shift the gulf stream, making northwestern Europe just as cold as Maine in winter.

year, and the prairies can get a lot less than this. From a point roughly halfway between the Rockies and the east coast, moist air from the Atlantic brings just enough rain to give trees the edge over grass, and the forest begins.

The temperate forest once covered virtually the whole of the eastern United States as well as parts of southeastern Canada. In the southeastern United States the climate is warm, wet, and almost frost-free, so the forest has an almost tropical feel. Farther north, the winter frosts get increasingly severe, so most of the forest trees are the deciduous type that grow fast in summer and lose their leaves in winter. Deciduous trees need to grow for at least four months of the year, but in the far north the summers are so short that this becomes impossible. So, north of the Canadian border, the deciduous trees gradually fade out, the northern evergreens take over, and the temperate forest gives way to taiga.

Atlantic Rain

Across the Atlantic, Europe has no spine of mountains acting as a barrier to moist ocean winds, so the climate is wet enough for temperate forest to grow almost all over the region. In Ireland and western Scotland there is enough rain throughout the year to support a temperate rain forest, but these countries lie

Deciduous trees look lifeless in winter, but the growing season in the temperate climate is long, and they will have time to regrow their leaves in spring.

15

Climographs

Each place in the world has its own pattern of weather. The typical pattern of weather that happens in one place during a year is called climate. We can sum up a place's climate on a climograph, such as the one shown here for St. Louis. The letters along the bottom are the months of the year. The numbers on the left and the small bars show rainfall, and the numbers on the right and the curvy line show temperature. You can see at a glance that St. Louis is hottest in July, but December is the driest month.

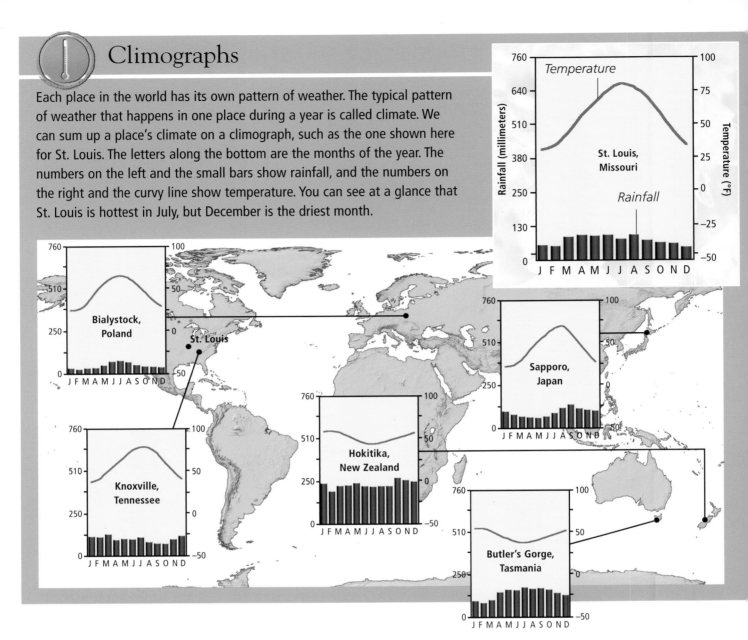

so far north that temperate evergreen trees cannot survive. Instead, the cool soils become waterlogged, which starves the ground of air and so stops dead plants from rotting away. The dead plants build up into masses of dead matter called peat bogs. Formed over thousands of years, these bogs once extended across large areas of Ireland and Scotland.

Farther east, where the rainfall is lighter but still reliable throughout the year, much of the land from Ireland to central Russia was originally covered in temperate deciduous forest, like the forests of New England. In the north this temperate forest grades into taiga, just as in Canada. To the south, around the Mediterranean, most of the rain falls in winter, and it may not rain at all in summer. This type of climate favors trees with tough, leathery evergreen leaves that can function in winter and resist drying out in summer. Where there is enough rain, these hardy trees sometimes form forests and woodlands, but most of the Mediterranean landscape is shrubland.

The Heart of Asia

Just beyond the Volga River, on the eastern fringes of Europe, the influence of the Atlantic Ocean finally fades. Denied the regular rainfall it needs, the temperate forest fizzles out in a scatter of trees and dry temperate grassland. This Asian equivalent of the North American prairie is known as steppe, and it extends across the heart of Asia to central China. To the north is the taiga forest, growing on land that, because of the long, dark winters, never really dries out. To the south is desert, much of it lying on the dry side of the Himalayas and the high plateau of Tibet. Far away from the gentle influence of the ocean, this northern desert and steppe is scorched in summer, bitterly cold in winter. It is among the last wildernesses on Earth.

To the **nomads** who still roam the central Asian heartlands, the steppe and desert must seem endless. But farther east the icy highlands of Tibet give way to the peaks and valleys of the central Chinese hill ranges, and the temperate zone comes under the influence of winds blowing off the Pacific Ocean. The climate is milder, with more reliable rainfall, and the forest can grow again.

This east Asian temperate forest region extends in a broad swath up to the Siberian border, and through Korea to Japan. On its southern fringes it is semitropical, while farther north the frosty winters favor deciduous trees, which shed their leaves in winter, mixed with evergreen conifers on poorer soils. But over the centuries, generations of farmers have stripped most of the trees from the Chinese lowlands. Today, the most extensive eastern temperate forests survive in the Siberian far east, Korea, and Japan. There, the rich colors of the deciduous trees in the fall recall those of New England, on the other side of the world.

The limestone pinnacles of southern China might make stunning scenery, but they don't make good farmland. So, they remain clothed in the temperate forest that covered much of China thousands of years ago.

FORESTS OF EUROPE

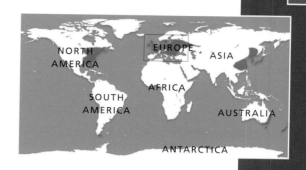

First settled by farmers in the Stone Age, about 9,000 years ago, the temperate deciduous forests of Europe have been cut and managed for millennia. Only fragments of the original wild forest remain, but the landscape is dotted with half-wild forests and small woodlands.

Forest Facts

▲ Crowded countries like the United Kingdom have lost most of their forest, but larger fragments of forest survive in the more thinly populated regions of the east, in countries like Romania. Even in France, forest still covers a quarter of the land.

▲ Before the last ice age, the forests of Europe and China may have formed a continuous belt.

▲ Temperate forests in eastern Europe are dying because of acid rain. The acid rain comes from pollution emitted from factories and power stations.

Bialowieza National Park

Perched on the border between Poland and Belarus, the Bialowieza Forest is a unique area of wilderness. It is part of the original untamed forest that once covered Europe from the Atlantic Ocean to the Ural Mountains. First protected as long ago as 1541, when it was a royal hunting ground, the forest is now protected by the United Nations as a Biosphere Reserve. This means hunting is banned.

Bialowieza is famous as a wild refuge for the European bison, or wisent, which was reintroduced after the last truly wild bison in the forest was shot by a poacher in 1919. Today there are more than 250 European bison roaming the forest, along with moose, beavers, lynx, and wolves.

1. Atlantic Ocean
The warm currents of the north Atlantic create the mild climate of western Europe. Temperate forest thrives in southern Sweden —that's as far north as southern Alaska.

2. The Pyrenees
This mountain barrier divides the deciduous temperate forests of central Europe from the hot, dry Mediterranean shrublands of Spain and Portugal. Fewer than 20 brown bears live in these mountains.

3. Fontainebleau
One of the earliest nature reserves in Europe, this former hunting forest has been protected since 1848.

4. Oberharz Nature Reserve
Centered in the Harz mountains, Oberharz is a relic of the dense forests that once covered central Germany. Many of its trees are damaged by acid rain.

5. The Alps
The soaring peaks and ridges of the Alps prevented plants spreading south in the last ice age, so many types became extinct. Glaciers in the Alps are shrinking because of global warming.

6. Bialowieza Forest
The largest surviving fragment of Europe's original wild forest, never cut or managed, except as a hunting ground. Pollution and logging are threats to wildlife in the forest.

7. Transylvanian Alps
These wild mountains are among the last haunts of European wolves. Bears and lynx live here, too.

8. Moscow
The Russian capital lies on the northern edge of the temperate forest zone. Air pollution affects Moscow.

9. Volga River
East of the mighty Volga, the forest fades into the steppes of central Asia. Fish, including sturgeon, are becoming rare as a result of industrial pollution in the river.

In early summer, before the forest trees have fully opened their leaves, bluebells carpet the ground in many British woodlands.

PLANTS OF THE FOREST

Trees like oaks, beeches, and maples dominate the world's biggest temperate forests. They are deciduous—they cope with winter by shedding their leaves in fall and growing new leaves in spring. The plants of the forest floor survive as roots, bulbs, or seeds, ready to shoot up from the ground in spring.

As it hurtles through space, taking spectacular photographs of the universe, the giant Hubble Space Telescope gets its power from the Sun. Solar panels soak up the light and convert it into electricity to drive the telescope's cameras and transmitters. Its batteries are always charged up because all its energy is supplied by the Sun.

Hundreds of kilometers below, on Earth, life also gets all its energy from the Sun. The chocolate bar that you eat to give you energy is made from cocoa beans and sugar, which come from plants. The plants make the sugar and the beans from simple chemicals that they absorb from the air and draw up through their roots. Like cooking, this process needs energy, and the plants get it by spreading their own solar panels—their leaves—in the sunlight.

The more light a leaf can collect, the better; so the best shape for the job is broad and flat. Besides absorbing energy, leaves have another function. Each leaf is peppered

with tiny holes, or pores, that let water **evaporate** and drift away. The process of evaporation makes the leaf suck in more water through its stalk. This, in turn, pulls water from the tree's twigs and branches, and up through its trunk from the roots—water

that carries vital chemicals the tree needs for making food. So leaves are not only energy-collecting solar panels; they also power the pumps that allow trees to collect chemicals from the ground.

Leaves for the Job

Around the equator, where it is always warm and wet, a leaf can do its job all year round. And since leaves are complicated structures, most tropical trees make them last as long as possible. Each leaf is thick and strong, and usually keeps working for a full year.

The trees that carry this type of leaf are called broad-leaved evergreens.

Many trees and smaller plants that live in other parts of the world use the same tactic, even though their leaves may be doing nothing for part of the year. In warmer temperate regions, like southern Australia and around the Mediterranean, the hot, dry summers are a problem for plants. If a plant

Evergreen rhododendrons dominate the foreground of this view of the Blue Ridge Parkway in the Appalachian Mountains. Behind is a mixture of broad-leaved trees, typical of temperate forests, and a few needle-leaved trees.

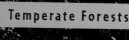

Unlike the temperate forest trees of Europe and North America, Australian eucalyptus trees keep their leaves throughout the year.

In **temperate** regions with harsh winters, such as the eastern United States, frost is the enemy. All plants contain a lot of water, and soft-stemmed plants keep themselves upright by filling their veins with water. This is why potted plants collapse if you forget to water them. They get into a far worse state if they are frozen, though.

When water turns into ice it expands and takes up more room. A lot of the water in a plant is inside tiny packages called cells—if it freezes and expands it can burst the cells and turn the plant tissue to mush. To see an example of this effect, try putting a fresh strawberry into the freezer.

Getting frozen like this can be deadly, but the plants of colder temperate forests have ways of defending themselves. One way is to grow strong, woody stems and extra-tough leaves that can survive being frozen. A few broad-leaved evergreen trees and shrubs, such as rhododendron and holly, use this method.

Holly leaves are thick, tough, and waterproof, like those of drought-resistant trees, and they live in the same warm, dry regions. But they are also tough enough to withstand freezing, and this allows holly to live in places with frosty winters. The leaves stay green all winter, which makes them a juicy target for browsing animals when there is not much else to eat. Holly trees protect themselves from being eaten with lower leaves that bristle with sharp spines.

Other evergreen trees have narrow, waxy leaves like needles or scales. These work well in droughts, which explains why needle-leaved conifers are common in dry places like the mountains of Nevada and California. They are also frost-proof, so they are perfect for trees growing in the far north, where the

keeps losing water from its leaves when there is no more in the soil to be sucked up by the roots, it will wilt and die.

Plants such as eucalyptus trees grow tough evergreen leaves with fewer pores than usual, so they lose far less water. The leaves are often waterproofed with wax, and they dangle or are held on edge instead of facing full sunshine. They don't work too well at catching light, but if there is a summer rainstorm they are ready to gather energy and pump water.

long winters favor trees such as pines and spruces. You can find out more about this type of forest in the *Taiga* book.

Shutdown

Tough-leaved evergreen trees like hollies and pines grow in all temperate forests, but they are not as successful as another group of trees that have developed a completely different way of dealing with winter. Instead of carrying small, thick, waterproof leaves that work relatively well all the time, the deciduous trees have broad, thin, delicate leaves that work very well for just some of the time. It's a gamble, but in a temperate climate it pays off.

Every spring, each deciduous tree grows a new set of these super-efficient leaves, and all summer they gather energy and pump water and **nutrients** to fuel the tree's chemical factories. They do their job so well that

Fire!

Every summer, ferocious wildfires sweep through vast areas of the world's temperate forests. Temperate forests in warmer places like southeast Australia are most at risk. In 2009, fires destroyed more than 4,500 square kilometers (1,700 square miles) of forest and farmland in the Australian state of Victoria.

An enormous fire like that is a disaster, but many of the trees in warm temperate forests need the occasional fire. Protected from the flames by their bark, the big trees survive while the blaze clears the ground of dead leaves and undergrowth. As the heat rises, it makes the cones and pods of the trees pop open, so their seeds fall out and drift down to the newly cleared ground—a perfect recipe for a brand-new crop of young trees.

These hazel twigs, although encased in ice, already have frost-proof leaf buds. Leaves will unfurl from the buds as soon as the ice melts in spring.

Spreading Seed

An oak tree can produce 90,000 acorns each year, but if these just fell straight to the ground they would have little chance of growing in their parent's shade. Even if they did grow, the saplings would steal food and water from their parent. So trees have found ways of scattering their seeds over wider areas, giving them a better chance to find a patch of sunlight in the forest.

Tiny birch seeds blow on the wind, while heavier maple seeds (right) have papery vanes that spin like the rotors of a helicopter to keep them airborne. Oaks make use of forest animals such as squirrels, jays, and chipmunks, which carry off the acorns for food, bury them, and then forget some. Other trees, such as hawthorns and cherries, have bright fruits that attract

birds. The birds swallow the fruits and digest the flesh, but the undamaged seeds pass through the birds, to be dumped on the other side of the forest.

a deciduous tree can grow much more efficiently than its evergreen neighbors. In most temperate forests, deciduous trees like oaks, beeches, maples, and aspens generally overwhelm the evergreens and crowd them out. The evergreens hang on in areas with bad soil, where deciduous trees have trouble getting enough plant food to make their new leaves each year.

The broad-leaved deciduous trees make the most of the warm summer by growing, flowering, and producing their seeds. As summer moves into winter, though, the failing light means that their leaves can make less and less food. If the weather gets really

Maple leaves burst from their buds in spring. At first tightly folded up, they soon flatten out and present their broad surfaces to the Sun.

cold, it doesn't rain but it snows, and the snow sits on the ground instead of soaking in. So in winter, the trees suffer as if there was a drought. The evergreens stick it out, but the deciduous trees shut down, dump all their leaves, and don't grow again until spring.

The Fall

Every leaf that a tree makes costs it energy. When a tree drops all its leaves at the end of the season, it throws away a big investment. To be sure of surviving—and doing better than the neighborhood evergreens—it must cut its losses. One of the most energy-expensive substances for a leaf to make is **chlorophyll**—the green chemical that captures sunlight and uses it to make sugar. Rather than lose all the valuable chlorophyll in its

American Forest Trees

The temperate forest biome in North America is not the same all over. In the north, in Quebec and Ontario, temperate forest gradually merges with the northern coniferous forest, or taiga. In the south, the temperate forest changes into exotic kinds of subtropical forests, where the evergreen trees have needle-shaped leaves to survive summer droughts, or have stilt roots to cope with living in swamps.

Maple; a typical broad-leaved deciduous tree of the temperate forest.

Red spruce; a typical needle-leaved, evergreen conifer tree of the taiga.

Loblolly pine; a needle-leaved, evergreen conifer of subtropical America.

leaves, a deciduous tree sucks it back into the twigs to be used again. As the green chemical drains from the leaves, they change color. In Europe most of the oaks, elms, beeches, chestnuts, and other trees turn brown or yellow, but in New England and Japan the forests are flushed with color as the maples turn bright gold and red.

When all the chlorophyll and **sap** has drained from each leaf, its stalk develops a thin layer of crumbly cork where it joins the twig. This is so brittle that a breath of wind is enough to snap the leaf away and send it fluttering to the ground. Within a few weeks,

Above: The leaves of deciduous trees, such as these maple leaves, turn different colors because they no longer contain the chlorophyll that made them green.

the forest is stripped bare, and the ground is hidden beneath a thick, multicolored carpet of shed leaves.

Without their leaves, the trees cannot make food. Trees have to save all their energy for spring, when they must somehow sprout a whole new set of leaves before they can start up the factory again. But they get a head start. Before the fall, each tree has already made its spring leaves, keeping them tightly packaged in frost-proof buds on every live twig. When the warm weather returns, the buds only have to pop open to allow the new leaves to unfurl and start working.

Dieback

The deciduous trees are the biggest, most noticeable plants in the temperate forest, but they are vastly outnumbered by the plants of the undergrowth. Most of these do not have tough, woody stems like the trees, and when winter arrives the frost destroys them.

Hearts of Oak

Trees like this mighty oak can grow to immense size because their trunks and branches are strengthened with tough, springy wood. Even in a live tree, most of this wood is dead, but it includes a thin living layer just below the bark. The living layer adds new sapwood to the trunk. Sapwood is a soft type of wood with veins that carry watery sap up from the tree's roots.

As the tree grows, it converts its inner sapwood to much harder, stronger heartwood, which supports the tree like a skeleton. The living tissue also produces another layer on its outside, which carries sugary sap down from the tree's leaves. Overlying this layer is the bark: a tough, corky sheath that protects the tree from frost, fire, and hungry animals.

Or at least, the plants seem to be destroyed. Their leaves and stems shrivel, collapse, and rot away.

But the plants are not dead. Like the deciduous trees, they are just shutting down for a while. As long as their roots are in good shape, they can survive having their foliage frozen and killed. They prepare for spring by building up food in bulbs, fleshy roots, or fat buds on the living parts just below ground level. The trees can help here as well, because a thick layer of fallen leaves on the forest floor acts like a blanket against the freezing air temperatures. When spring arrives, new green shoots sprout through the fallen leaves, and the plants that appeared dead are back in business.

Below: In North America, trilliums grow on the forest floor and can live there for many years. Like trees, their underground bulbs lay down a ring of growth every year.

Plants that die back in winter but survive underground are known as herbaceous perennials. **Herbaceous plants** die down to ground level each winter, and **perennial** plants keep going year after year. Herbaceous perennials do both. They are particularly common in temperate deciduous forests, because when the trees are still without leaves in early spring, the forest floor is flooded with light. This gives small plants a chance to grow, flower, and spread beneath the trees—but only if they are ready and waiting to sprout from just below the surface.

This spring surge of growth creates some of the most spectacular flower shows on Earth. In the deciduous woods of Virginia and North Carolina, great drifts of violets, blue delphiniums, and white trillium lilies burst into bloom, soaking up sunshine so they can make their seeds before they are shaded by the new tree foliage. In Europe, and especially in England, the woods are carpeted with a magical haze of bluebells, along with wood anemones, daffodils, and primroses. You can see wood anemones drinking in the energy of the light, as each flower tracks the movement of the Sun through the sky like a tiny dish antenna.

Living in the Shade

The spring flowers have to race to set their seeds, because by early summer the sunlight is blocked out by the spreading canopy of leaves on the forest trees. The trilliums and bluebells soon vanish beneath a dense growth of nettles, ferns, and other plants that flourish in shade. These have broad leaves that are well suited to gathering as much light as possible, so the plants can make food. But there is another way a plant can get food while living in the shade: It can steal it.

One of the plants that grows in European forests is a delicate-looking flower called cow wheat. Although it has slender leaves, which capture only a little sunlight to make food, it can live in deep shade. It survives because it attaches its roots to those of other plants and steals their sugary sap. It lives off others in the same way that bloodsucking animals such as ticks and lice do. These freeloading animals

 ## Clues from Rings

When a tree is growing fast in spring and early summer, it adds a thick layer of wood to its trunk. In late summer, it grows more slowly, adding a thinner, harder layer, then stops altogether. In spring it starts up again, adding another thick layer. By counting the layers, which show as rings on the cut end of a felled tree, you can work out the age of the tree. The layers also record the weather during the tree's lifetime. A good summer creates a thick layer, while a cold summer results in a thin one. The rings of very old trees can show climatologists what conditions were like during periods of climate change in the past, such as during the Little Ice Age in the 17th and 18th centuries, C.E.

Prickly Survivor

The first seed-producing trees appeared on Earth about 300 million years ago. They were primitive, scaly versions of modern conifers like pines and spruces, and they dominated the forests for about a hundred million years until the ancestors of today's broad-leaved trees started taking over.

Amazingly, a few of these primitive types of trees still grow in temperate forests. The most spectacular is the monkey puzzle or Chile pine (left), which has sharp scales instead of leaves, and grows up to 30 meters (100 feet) tall on the slopes of volcanoes in the southern Andes mountains. Barely changed in 200 million years, it probably developed its spiny defenses to discourage hungry dinosaurs!

Left: Fungi get their food in an amazing range of ways, but in a temperate forest you can often find them feeding on dead wood.

and plants are called parasites. Weird-looking parasitic plants called broomrapes go further than cow wheat, and get all their food from the roots of other plants. Since they make no food of their own, they do not need chlorophyll. So instead of being green, they are almost colorless. Some orchids live in a similar way, and can survive in virtual darkness.

Yet the real experts at getting food without light are the strange organisms we call fungi. A **fungus** is not a plant. It is mostly made of chitin, which is the material that forms the

Below: Mushrooms and toadstools come in different shapes and colors. A few, such as these fly agaric toadstools, are brightly colored. The color may warn animals that the fungus is poisonous.

hard outer casing of insects. Instead of making its own food from raw chemicals, as green plants do, a fungus eats ready-made food, like dead plants or animals. A fungus can dissolve wood and turn it into sugar, which it then uses to make its own structure. And like broomrape, some fungi are parasites that eat live food.

The fungi most of us know about are the various sorts of mushrooms that pop up overnight from the forest floor, but these are just the fruits of much bigger organisms that live hidden in the soil. Their threadlike stems form tangled mats that gather food from decaying leaves or rotting timber. These often cover huge areas—scientists investigating a honey fungus growing in a temperate forest in Michigan found that it extended over 125,000 square meters (150,000 square yards)—the size of a small airfield.

The threads of some fungi also entwine the roots of living plants and steal some of their sap. Yet the plants can survive this, because some fungi repay the plants by supplying certain substances that plants cannot get from the soil by themselves. Many of the plants in temperate forests rely on these partnerships for survival—if their seedlings are planted in soil that does not contain the right sort of fungus, they keel over and die.

Windows of Opportunity

Although the forest plants put a lot of effort into producing seeds, most of them never get a chance to grow. The ground is too crowded, and there is often not enough light for tiny seedlings to get a good start. They need a break, and they get one if a big tree is blown over in a storm. This makes a clearing in the forest, letting in the light. It gives the seeds the chance that they have been waiting for.

The ghost orchid of European temperate forests is white because it doesn't need chlorophyll to make its own food. Like a fungus, it feeds on dead leaves.

First to start growing are the fast-breeding plants like foxglove and willowherb. Within a few weeks, the bare ground is thick with them, and for a year or two their flowers form a bright splash of sunlit color in the forest. Meanwhile, other seeds have been blown in on the wind, such as those of birch trees. These also sprout in the sunlit clearing, and after a few years the young birch trees shade out the earlier arrivals and grow into a small birch thicket.

Birches do not live long, though. Eventually they give way to trees such as oaks, maples, and tulip trees. And so, after many years, the wound in the forest heals over.

NEW ZEALAND

Strange prehistoric trees, such as podocarps and tree ferns, make up the temperate rain forest of New Zealand. People cut down most of the forest hundreds of years ago, but patches survive to this day.

The spreading crowns of podocarp trees give the temperate rain forest a tropical look.

Bird Islands

Isolated in the southern Pacific for 80 million years, the landmass of New Zealand has been cut off from the rest of the world since the time of the dinosaurs. As a result, there were no ground-living mammals on the islands until people arrived and introduced some animals about 1,000 years ago. Birds, however, could reach New Zealand by flying. Over millions of years of evolution, they took over all the roles normally played by mammals. Well-known birds of New Zealand include kiwis, five species of insect-eating flightless birds which feed by night, probing and sniffing the soft soil for insects and earthworms, and kakapos, plant-eating parrots, again nocturnal and flightless.

Kiwis and kakapos are threatened with extinction. However, there are ongoing conservation efforts to save them. For example, In the late 1980s, all New Zealand's kakapos (about 40) were rounded up and relocated on Codfish Island, off South Island, which had been cleared of introduced predators, such as weasels and foxes. By 2009, the number of these parrots had risen to 124. The New Zealand government takes measures to protect its native species. Visitors' bags and clothing are searched for non-native animals and plants, which may overrun fragile habitats. In addition, introduced animals such as weasels, stoats, and feral ferrets, which were originally released to control another introduced animal—the rabbit—are routinely trapped or shot.

N

Tasman Sea

ASIA

AUSTRALIA

ANTARCTICA

1. Auckland
The chief port and industrial center of New Zealand, and its largest city.

2. Rotorua
This volcanic area of North Island is famous for its hot springs and geysers. Cats and dogs threaten native animals.

3. Lake Taupo
The central lake of North Island is surrounded by forested mountain wildlife reserves. Fertilizers washing into the lake disrupts aquatic life.

4. Mount Egmont
Although now extinct, Mount Egmont, or Taranaki, is the biggest of many volcanoes on North Island.

5. Wellington
The capital city of New Zealand, overlooking an ocean passage named Cook Strait.

6. Southern Alps
Most of the surviving temperate rain forest is on the slopes of these mountains.

7. Christchurch
The main city of South Island, on the edge of the fertile Canterbury Plains.

8. Canterbury Plains
One of the earliest areas to be cleared of forest by the Maori people, more than 500 years ago.

9. Fiordland National Park
The wildest corner of New Zealand, and a spectacular haven for wildlife. Its southern beech and podocarp forests shelter rare species of parrots, skinks, and unique New Zealand birds. Areas of the park may soon be opened up for mining.

10. Stewart Island
Although swept by the winds that howl around Antarctica, the southern-most part of New Zealand has dense temperate rain forests. The survival of the Stewart Island shag is threatened by introduced cats and weasels.

Ninety Mile Beach

NORTHLAND

Great Barrier Island

Hanauraki Gulf

Auckland
[1]

Coromandel Peninsula

Bay of Plenty

Waikato River

Hamilton

Raukumara Range

East Cape

[2] !

Rotorua

Lake Taupo

[3] !

Mount Egmont
[4]

Mount Ruapehu

Hawke Bay

North Island

Ruahine Range

NEW

ZEALAND

Cook Strait

miles   kilometers
100
100
0   0

Tasman Bay

Tasman Mths.

Wellington
[5]

Pacific Ocean

Kaikoura Ranges

Hokitika

Southern Alps

South Island

[6]

Christchurch
[7]

Canterbury Plains

[8]

Mount Cook

Mount Aspiring

Waitaki River

Lake Wakatipu

OTAGO

Pacific Ocean

Lake Te Anau

Fiordland

[9]
!

SOUTHLAND

Dunedin

Catlins

Invercargill

Stewart Island

[10] !

Fact File

▲ More than 150 million years ago, New Zealand was part of a gigantic continent called Gondwana, which slowly broke apart. The rain forest here is all that is left of the vast prehistoric forest that covered Gondwana.

▲ Dinosaurs once lived in forests like New Zealand's. Podocarp trees and tree ferns probably provided food for plant-eating dinosaurs.

▲ Similar forests grow in Tasmania and southern Chile. They used to cover Antarctica, too, until it drifted so far south that it froze solid.

33

ANIMALS OF THE FOREST

Temperate forests teem with animals, from leaf-nibbling insects to wolves and bears. But when the trees lose their leaves in winter, food is hard to find and life becomes tough. To survive, animals must make the most of the changing seasons.

If you stand under an oak tree on a warm day in early summer and look up, you might think it's raining. The air is full of drops of moisture, falling on your face. But the drops are not water. They are honeydew: a sticky, sugary fluid ejected by sap-sucking bugs feeding high in the tree. These bugs swarm over the leaves in the thousands, filling their tiny bodies with sweet sap. Every now and then, each bug produces a tiny bead of surplus sugar and water and lets it fall. There are so many bugs in the tree that the honeydew falls like continuous light rain. The whole tree is literally crawling with life.

A single European oak can provide food for more than 1,000 different types of insects, including 45 sorts of sap-sucking bugs and more than 200 varieties of caterpillars. They drink the sap, munch through the leaves, and nibble the buds. Tough-jawed beetle grubs gnaw into the bark and timber, and long-nosed weevils drill into acorns to lay their eggs. All these insects are hunted by an army of wasps and spiders, and these, in turn, are snapped up by small birds that nest in the branches.

Chipmunks are good climbers, but they spend most of their time on the ground searching for food. They bury secret stores of nuts and seeds around the forest to eat in winter.

Treecreepers (right) spiral up tree trunks, using their tweezer bills to pick out small insects. Meanwhile, heavy-billed woodpeckers drill for wood-boring grubs, like that of the stag beetle (inset), which grows to 10 centimeters (4 inches) long.

Bigger birds, like pigeons and crows, raid the tree for acorns, and when the ripe acorns fall they are eagerly gathered by mice, squirrels, and deer.

And that's just one tree. A small wood contains hundreds of such trees, and a forest has thousands. Growing up to 30 meters (100 feet) tall, they form a huge, living, three-dimensional home for countless wild animals. But there is a catch, and it happens every year: winter.

Hard Times

In the tropical rain forest, there is no winter. Rain-forest animals can feed and breed all year round, and flourish in such colossal numbers that they probably outweigh all the other animals on land. But temperate forests are not

like that. However lush and green the trees are in summer, winter transforms them into dead-looking skeletons.

They are not usually dead, of course, and there is food to be had if you know where to look, but not enough to feed the teeming populations of animals that live in the rain forest. So any animal that wants to enjoy summer in the temperate forest has to find a way of coping with winter.

Eurasian lynx once lived throughout the temperate forests of Europe and Asia, but today they are more common in the taiga, where there are fewer people to hunt and kill them. People are now releasing lynx into the temperate forests of countries like France, Germany, and the Czech Republic to reestablish them there. Lynx prey on small animals such as mice, rabbits, and birds, as well as the occasional deer.

To survive in a temperate forest, an animal has to change its way of life with the seasons. It cannot develop a specialty like eating ants, because ants are simply not available for half the year. That's why there are no dedicated anteaters in temperate forests.

In tropical forests, trees can bear fruit at any time of year. Whole flocks of fruit bats spend their time searching for these trees, and when they finish feeding in one tree, they look for another. They can carry on like that all year. But in the temperate forest, all the trees that bear fruit do it at the end of summer. For a few weeks, there is plenty of fruit for all, but then it's gone. An animal that eats fruit and nothing else would be in big trouble; unsurprisingly, there are no fruit bats in the temperate forests.

Instead, the fruit is eaten by generalists—animals that eat lots of different things. An American black bear, for example, may spend up to 20 hours a day feasting on berries and apples in fall, along with acorns, beech nuts, insects, dead meat, and any small animals it can catch. The fruit comes in very handy, because it is full of energy that the bear can store as fat to keep it going through winter. Badgers do much the same, gorging themselves in a race to put on as much weight as possible before the food runs out. Squirrels, chipmunks, and jays gather nuts and seeds with feverish speed and hide them in secret stores to eat later. Throughout the forest, the fruit and nut season is a time of urgent activity, because the animals know that hard times are on the way.

The Big Sleep

A black bear has a simple way of getting through the winter. Having stuffed itself with so much food that it puts on a 13-centimeter (5-inch) layer of fat around its body, it looks for a snug den in a cave or hollow tree. When it finds one, it goes to sleep.

It sleeps much more deeply than normal, though. All its body processes—its heart rate, breathing, digestion, and body chemistry (**metabolism**)—slow down. Its temperature also falls a little, from 38°C (100°F) to maybe 31°C (88°F). In this state, the bear's body uses less energy than when it is active, so its store of fat lasts longer. In the long, cold

 Gone Forever

The laughing owl, named for its mischievous-sounding call, lived in New Zealand. It grew up to 40 centimeters (16 inches) in height and had a wingspan up to 53 centimeters (21 inches). Different types, or subspecies, lived in forests on both the North and South Islands of New Zealand. They ate insects, lizards, and the kiore—or Polynesian rat—and later mice, which were introduced by European settlers. These owls preferred to chase down prey on the ground, rather than hunt on the wing. The laughing owl became extinct in the early 1900s, falling prey to predatory animals, such as cats and stoats, which were brought to New Zealand by the Europeans.

winters of northern Minnesota, black bears may have to survive like this for more than six months, so every little bit helps.

Squirrels and badgers sleep through the winter in much the same way, although since squirrels cannot put on so much fat, they often wake up to raid their stores of nuts. They are lucky, because nuts keep well through winter. Other small animals are not so fortunate. Unless they can escape winter altogether by flying away to somewhere warm, they have to survive the long, cold months without any food. They do this by falling into a much deeper kind of sleep called **hibernation**.

A European hedgehog, for example, eats mainly worms, insects, slugs, and similar small animals, but such prey is extremely hard to find in winter. So, like the black bear, it stuffs itself with food before the cold weather arrives. Then it curls up and goes to sleep, often in a pile of fallen leaves on the forest floor. Sleep is hardly the right word, though, because its body almost shuts down

altogether. Its temperature can fall to near freezing, and its heart rate and breathing slow to the point where it seems to be dead. In this state, its body uses so little energy that a well-fed hedgehog can get through winter without eating at all—although it will be very thin by the time it wakes up in spring.

Chilling Out

Animals such as frogs, snakes, and butterflies have no option but to hibernate, because they rely on the Sun to keep them warm. They are often called "cold-blooded," but this is confusing because in summer their blood is as warm as ours, and maybe warmer. When they are warm their muscles work well and they can digest food properly. But when winter arrives, they are forced to slow down, switch off, and chill out.

Frogs often hibernate on the bottoms of forest pools beneath the ice; provided the water doesn't freeze solid, the frogs survive. Forest snakes go underground, hiding in burrows or cavities beneath tree roots. Sometimes several hundred American garter snakes hibernate in a single den, knotted together in an effort to keep out the worst

 Drumbeat

In spring, the temperate forests ring with birdsong, but one sort of song is quite unlike the others. It's a mechanical, drumming rattle that sounds like a miniature road drill: the song of a woodpecker.

Woodpeckers are equipped with strong, sharp bills for hammering at timber, to get at wood-boring insect grubs and to excavate nest holes. In spring, they make the most of this pecking power by drumming on dead branches to attract mates. Every bird takes care to select a drum with good ringing tone, and each type of woodpecker has its own special drumming style.

Beware the Bear

A sleeping black bear might look like a big, cuddly toy, but it certainly isn't. Even in the middle of winter, a bear can wake up from a deep sleep in just a few moments, and although black bears don't eat people, they really hate being disturbed. Startled bears quickly become angry bears, and an angry bear is something you don't want to meet. It might just smack you with a paw before it lumbers off into the forest, but even a quick swipe of those can-opener claws is enough to do considerable damage. You don't mess with bears.

The Great Escape

Most seed-eating birds can find enough food in the temperate forest to see them through the winter, but for insect eaters and nectar feeders, life becomes impossible. The little ruby-throated hummingbird (right), for example, breeds throughout the forests of the eastern United States in summer. Like all hummingbirds, it feeds mainly on nectar, hovering on whirring wings to sip from its favorite red flowers. It also eats a few insects. Both nectar and insects are impossible to find in winter, so the hummingbird flies south to Central America. To get there, it crosses the Gulf of Mexico in a nonstop flight of 800 kilometers (500 miles)—an amazing feat for a tiny bird.

The same crossing is made by larger red-eyed vireos and scarlet tanagers. These insect- and fruit-eating birds of the northeastern temperate forests fly all the way to South America for the winter, traveling up to 10,000 kilometers (6,000 miles) in total. In Europe, the little willow warbler may migrate the same distance from English woodland to southern Africa, and return to exactly the same woods the following spring.

NORTH AMERICA

EUROPE

ASIA

CENTRAL AMERICA

ruby-throated hummingbird's route

SOUTH AMERICA

willow warbler's route

AFRICA

of the cold. Even so, if the temperature in the den drops below freezing point, the snakes can freeze, too. This is usually fatal, but not always. A garter snake can survive freezing for a few hours, even if nearly half its body fluids turn to ice.

Some cold-blooded animals have an antifreeze chemical in their bodies that stops water from turning into ice. These include many butterflies that spend the winter as pupae—the transition stage when a caterpillar turns into an adult. The pupae attach themselves to trees and sit tight,

European dormice hibernate for about seven months in a nest of dead leaves underground. While hibernating, they become as cold as their surroundings.

Black rat snakes live in the temperate forests of North America. In addition to rats, they prey on squirrels, chipmunks, birds, birds' eggs, and other snakes.

surviving temperatures that plunge well below freezing. In spring, they hatch as winged adults, none the worse for their deep-freeze experience.

Other forest insects cannot survive winter and are killed by the cold weather. To a tiny insect, a single summer is a long time—certainly long enough for it to find a mate and produce some eggs. Protected by their shells, the eggs are much tougher than the insects that laid them, and are able to withstand hard frosts. They hatch in spring, producing an army of grubs and caterpillars just as the forest trees sprout their new leaves. In summer, these infant insects turn into adults, which mate, lay eggs, and die in fall, completing the cycle.

Most forest animals try to live longer than a single summer. If they can't avoid winter by hibernating, they have another option—they can go somewhere warmer. When spring arrives and the forest bursts back into life, the animals return. This regular movement with the seasons is called migration, and the most seasoned travelers are birds.

Cold Comfort

In fall, millions of birds migrate south to find food in the tropics. Meanwhile, the northern temperate forest is gripped by winter. Most of the shrubs and trees are bare, but their buds—and the insect eggs that often lie inside them—make good eating for the small birds that stay behind.

Below them, the fallen leaves lie in deep layers, because the cold weather slows the activity of the tiny animals and fungi that will eventually eat the leaves and convert them into soil. This is good news for mice and voles. They tunnel beneath the

 Tiny Terrors

The scariest animals of the temperate forest are not bears, or even wolves. They are tiny animals called ticks, which climb onto your skin and suck your blood. You might think this is no big deal, and in a way you'd be right—no tick can steal more than a pea-sized drop of blood. But what they give you in return for the meal can be deadly.

Ticks carry more nasty microorganisms than any other type of bug, and the microorganisms cause horrible diseases. Among the diseases spread by ticks are Rocky Mountain spotted fever, Colorado tick fever, and Lyme disease. Lyme disease is one of the fastest-growing infectious diseases in the United States. Its symptoms include a fever, a headache, tiredness, and a rash. If left untreated, Lyme disease may cause severe joint problems.

insulating blanket of leaves and snow to nibble at scattered seeds and nuts, and never need to emerge into the cold winter air.

Larger animals must endure the cold, however. As they burn energy trying to keep warm, they get hungrier than ever. In European forests, wild boar grub among the leaves looking for acorns and roots. Birds follow them to snatch up any worms or insects that get unearthed. Deer and bison kick the snow aside in search of greenery, but often resort to eating twigs and bark. In the misty forests of China, giant pandas may abandon their usual diet of bamboo shoots to scavenge the carcasses of animals that have died from cold and starvation.

All the while, there is danger. Agile forest hawks, like the European sparrowhawk and American sharp-shinned hawk, swoop and swerve through the bare branches to seize small birds in midair. These are hunted in turn by more powerful killers, like the northern goshawk. At night, owls listen for mice scurrying through the leaf litter, then glide down on soundless wings to snatch them up in their talons. Red foxes and even wolves prowl the forest in search of prey or dead meat, while beneath the snow, slender weasels chase voles through their runs and burrows. Deeper still, moles tunnel in the soil, devouring worms and fat beetle grubs.

Hungry Hordes

As the days get longer in spring, the buds on the trees swell and burst, and new leaves unfurl in the sunshine. At the same time, all the insect eggs that have weathered the winter in buds and bark crevices hatch out, and swarms of caterpillars and other grubs emerge to nibble the tender young foliage.

Roe deer are common in European forests. Always on the lookout for danger, they bark like dogs when alarmed. The males regrow their antlers every spring.

Long Haul

Butterflies look too fragile to go on long migrations, but some do exactly that. The most traveled are the monarch butterflies that spend summer in the temperate forests around North America's Great Lakes. Rather than risk freezing in the northern winter, many fly southwest on an awesome 3,200-kilometer (2,000-mile) journey to Mexico. There they roost in the millions in a few trees that have been used by their ancestors for centuries (right). They rest until spring, then fly north again— over several generations—to the Great Lakes.

Sometimes insects attack a tree in such numbers that they strip all its leaves. Unable to make food, the tree stops growing, and may even die if insects attack it year after year. The most notorious of these hungry hordes are caterpillars of the gypsy moth, which attack oaks, aspens, and similar trees. In its native Europe, birds and predatory insects keep the gypsy moth in check. In the 1860s, however, people accidentally released the gypsy moth in North America, where it had no natural enemies. It has spread throughout the northeastern United States and regularly destroys huge areas of forest.

Normally, as the insects feed and grow fat, they attract insect-eating birds. Many birds will have stayed in the forest all winter, but they are soon joined by migrants returning to feast on the insects and raise their families. The forest bursts into song as the male birds stake their claims to desirable nesting sites, warn off rivals, and try to attract females.

Once their eggs hatch, the birds face the challenge of feeding the hungry youngsters. Baby birds need high-**protein** food if they are

to grow properly, so even seed-eating birds like finches feed their nestlings on caterpillars and other insects. Meanwhile, bigger birds, such as hawks and crows, are feeding their young, too. With the forest full of eggs and nestlings, they enjoy rich pickings. Luckily, if small birds lose their first family to predators, they normally have enough time to start a second one.

Birds are not the only animals feasting on the insects. In the forests of southeastern Australia and Tasmania, sap-eating animals called sugar gliders switch their attention to caterpillars, beetles, and small spiders in the spring. The protein-rich diet helps them build up strength for the breeding season.

In spring, scarlet tanagers fly from the rain forests of South America to eastern North America to raise families. Their favorite nesting sites are oak trees.

Sugar gliders are also known as flying possums. They make their way from tree to tree by leaping across open spaces, high above the forest floor, and gliding on furry webs of skin stretched between their outspread legs. They can travel up to 100 meters (330 feet) like this, saving them the trouble—and risk—of coming down to the ground. They are only active at night, and have huge eyes that gather the dim light and pick out their target trees in the gloom.

While gliders find their way in the dark by sight, insect-eating bats orient by sound. As it hunts, a bat emits a rapid stream of squeaks. These spread out through the air like ripples on a pond, and bounce off trees, leaves, and airborne insects. The bat's sensitive ears pick up these echoes and convert them into a stream of electrical nerve signals, rather like the signals that pour down a cable TV line. The bat's brain then

A sugar glider uses its bushy tail as a rudder while gliding between trees. It has sharp claws and a pincerlike grip for holding on when it lands.

 ## Bamboo Bear

Bears are basically meat eaters that have developed a taste for eating fruit, nuts, sugary sap, and other vegetable foods. But one bear—the giant panda—lives almost entirely on the grass bamboo.

Giant pandas live in the mountain forests of central China, on the fringes of Tibet. There, the tall trees rise above a dense undergrowth of bamboo, which grows so thick that the panda never has to look far for a meal. An average panda has to eat about 8 kilograms (18 pounds) of bamboo every day. That's like eating about 16 big packages of breakfast cereal! Even so, the energy from the bamboo is barely enough to cover the giant panda's daily needs. So, unlike a black bear, the panda can't put on enough weight to sleep through the winter. It has to stay awake—and keep eating. About 1,400 pandas lived in the wild. Fragmentation and loss of their bamboo habitat threaten their survival.

The damp forest floor is a perfect home for salamanders, which need to stay moist. In recent years, fungal disease has wiped out many populations of salamanders.

builds up an image from the signals, just like the TV, so the bat can see in the dark. This way of "seeing" is called echolocation.

Most forest bats hunt flying insects such as moths and beetles, using echolocation to capture them as they flit and drone through the night air. But a European long-eared bat has such sensitive hearing that it can hear the faint footsteps made by prey crawling and fluttering over leaves and branches. Flying with amazing precision, it weaves its way slowly through the foliage, scanning for juicy prey lurking among the leaves. When it detects a suitable victim, it hovers, pinpoints the source of the sound, and then seizes the insect—and all in complete darkness.

Return Flight

As summer wears on, the leaves on the trees get darker, tougher, and less edible. Most of the insect grubs have turned into moths, wasps, and flies, so the feeding frenzy slows down. Many adult insects do not eat at all but live just long enough to mate and lay eggs. Their job done, they run out of energy and are picked off by birds and bats, or simply fall exhausted to the forest floor.

With fewer insects to catch, many of the birds that flew north from the tropics in spring get ready to fly back again. To be sure of making the trip, they eat ravenously in late summer to build up big stores of energy-rich fat, making the most of the insects while they last. Some migrant birds may leave the northern temperate forests as early as August. In more southerly forests, they hang on as late as October. Eventually, all the summer visitors disappear, and as the leaves start falling from the trees, the animals that are left behind prepare for another winter.

The long-eared bat's sensitive ears can hear the tiniest rustle among the leaves of an oak tree. After snatching its meal, the bat returns to a perch to feed at leisure.

45

JAPAN

Japan is a land of rugged mountain ranges and rocky islands. Since most people live near the coasts, the mountains are still heavily forested. Many of the original trees have been replaced by conifer plantations, but patches of native temperate forest survive.

1. Hokkaido
The cold northern island of Japan is like neighboring Siberia, with large areas of evergreen taiga forest. Hunting and poaching of brown bears put this animal at risk. In recent years, efforts have been made to save the Japanese red-crowned crane.

2. Akan National Park
One of many national parks in Japan, but designed for leisure rather than nature conservation. Pollution and poaching of sables are problems in the park.

3. Towada-Hachimantai
This national park has volcanoes, hot springs, lakes, and valleys forested with beech trees.

Fact File

▲ Many of Japan's 3,000 islands have formed within the last few thousand years from volcanoes growing from the ocean floor.

▲ Large areas of native temperate forest survived in Japan until recently, but over the last 50 years they have been replanted with conifer trees or cleared to make room for industrial development.

▲ Today, many Japanese forests are protected from loggers. But people still need wood, and demand for timber is met by countries such as Malaysia, where logging companies are cutting down the wild forests.

▲ There are still inaccessible areas in Japan, such as parts of Hokkaido (left), where mountain torrents rush through forested valleys.

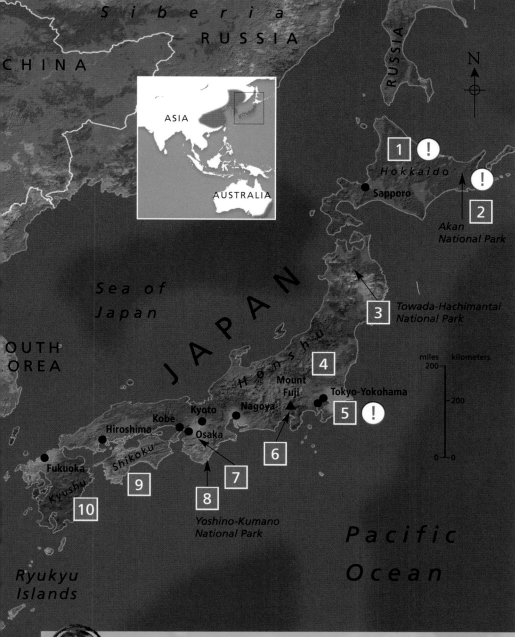

CHINA
RUSSIA
Siberia
ASIA
AUSTRALIA
RUSSIA

N

☐1 ❗

Hokkaido

● Sapporo

❗
☐2

Akan National Park

Sea of Japan

JAPAN

☐3 Towada-Hachimantai National Park

Honshu

☐4

Mount Fuji

Tokyo-Yokohama

☐5 ❗

SOUTH KOREA

Kyoto
Kobe
● Nagoya
Hiroshima
Osaka
Shikoku
☐6

☐9
☐7

Fukuoka
Kyushu
☐8

☐10

Yoshino-Kumano National Park

Ryukyu Islands

Pacific Ocean

miles | kilometers
200 —
— 200
0 — 0

4. Honshu
The main island, densely populated around the coasts but with forested highlands inland.

5. Tokyo-Yokohama
One of the biggest urban areas in the world, with 30 million people —equaling the entire population of Canada. Air pollution is a problem in such a huge city.

6. Mount Fuji
The symbol of Japan, Fuji is just one of many volcanoes that have created the rugged Japanese landscape.

7. Osaka
The second largest population center in Japan. Neighboring Kobe was destroyed by a devastating earthquake in January 1995.

8. Yoshino-Kumano
This national park includes mountains and forests where bears, wild sheep, and rare types of woodland salamanders live.

9. Shikoku
The smallest of Japan's main islands, separated from Honshu by an inland sea.

10. Kyushu
The main southern island, where the temperate forest merges into subtropical rain forest.

Snow Monkeys

The Japanese macaque is the only monkey that lives in deciduous temperate forest. Most monkeys live in the tropics, where they can eat fruit all year round, but Japanese macaques have discovered other foods such as leaves, crop plants, potatoes, insects, and small animals. They find most of their food on the ground, often digging it out of the snow in winter. Their extra-thick coats help them survive the cold, and in volcanic regions where there are hot springs, they keep warm by spending lots of time in warm pools.

FORESTS AND PEOPLE

More people live in the temperate forest biome than in any other, and this is no coincidence. The fertile soil, enriched by the yearly leaf fall, is perfect for agriculture.

Around 10,000 years ago, someone had the bright idea of attaching a stone blade to the end of a long wooden handle. The result was an ax. The blade was nothing new—people had been making and using stone tools for thousands of years. But the handle made a huge difference. Instead of chipping away with a rock held in the fist, a person could swing the rock to strike a target with shattering force. Suddenly it was possible to chop through the trunk of a mighty tree like an oak. For many of the world's temperate forests, it was the beginning of the end.

Over the next few thousand years, vast areas of temperate forest were cleared. The felled trees were used for fuel and timber, and the land for farming. At first, the farmers may have worked the land for a few years and

A satellite took this picture of electric lights at night. Compare it with the map on pages 6–7 and you'll notice that most of the light comes from areas of temperate forest. That's because the temperate forest biome has a more dense human population than any other.

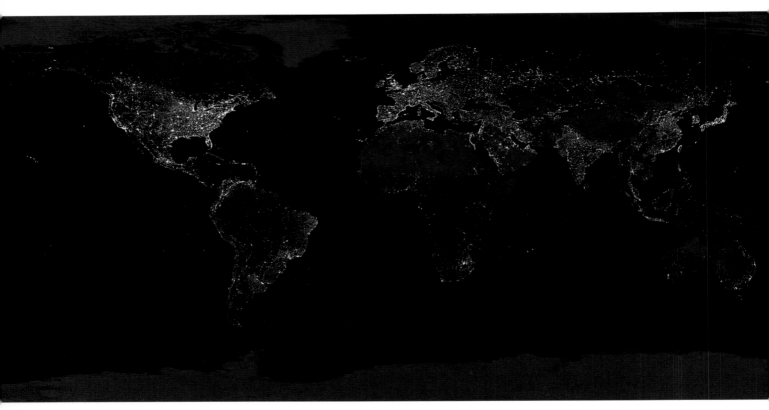

Public Enemy

For thousands of years, the temperate forests of the north echoed to the howling of wolves. Wolf packs roamed the whole of North America, Europe, and northern Asia, through woodlands, prairies, and deserts. When people started keeping sheep and other livestock, wolves became public enemy number one, and they were ruthlessly slaughtered. Too big to hide in open country, the wolves retreated to the forests. But as the temperate forests dwindled, the wolves vanished. Today, they live mainly in the dark taiga forests of the north. In recent years, wolves have been reintroduced by government agencies into certain forests in the United States.

then moved on, allowing the forest to grow again. But mostly they stayed, because they had discovered something worth staying for—rich, **fertile** soil.

Rich Soil

To grow decent crops, you need rich soil. But if you keep harvesting plants from the same patch of ground, year after year, the soil loses its richness, or fertility. Soil gets its fertility from dead plants and animals. As these rot and break down, they release chemicals called nutrients, which plants need. When the nutrients get used up, the soil becomes infertile, and plants grow much more slowly.

Fertility runs out especially fast on farms in tropical rain forests. Dead plants and animals decay quickly in the hot, wet climate. This converts them into nutrients, and the trees absorb these almost right away. If the trees are felled and trucked away, they take the nutrients with them.

In a temperate forest, the thick layers of leaves dumped in fall decay much more slowly. In winter, the cold preserves them, and the decaying process only gets going in spring and summer. Fungi, bacteria, and tiny creatures break the leaves into smaller and smaller particles that get washed deep into the ground by rain. Earthworms plow through the earth and churn it up, creating a fertile layer of mineral grains and slowly rotting leaf fragments.

The nutrients in this soil are released much more slowly than in a rain forest, and plants absorb them more slowly, too. This means that if the trees are cut down and cleared away, there are enough nutrients left for many, many years of simple farming. And if farmers allow animals onto the land from time to time to enrich the soil with manure, they can grow crops indefinitely. So the soils of the temperate forest biome make some of the best farmland in the world.

The First Farmers

Some of the first people to discover the rich soils of the temperate forests were **Stone Age** farmers, who moved into Europe from the eastern Mediterranean about 9,000 years ago. At first, these newcomers kept their farming skills to themselves, while the original inhabitants stuck to hunting, fishing, and gathering wild food. But gradually, most of the peoples of Europe became farmers, and by about 6,000 years ago, there were farmsteads dotted all over Europe.

Even so, most of the original temperate forest was still standing 6,000 years ago, and it stayed standing for at least another 3,000 years. Scientists know this from studies of pollen—the tiny dustlike particles released from flowers. Studies of ancient layers of soil have revealed large amounts of tree pollen,

proving that the forests still existed. The ancient farmers probably valued the forest as a source of food and timber.

They soon discovered that if they cut down trees such as ash and hazel and left the stumps behind, each stump would sprout five or more new shoots that were just the right size for firewood, fence posts, house building, and even road making. Scientists have found 6,000-year-old roads across English marshland made entirely from these poles.

Instead of felling all the big forest trees for timber—no easy job with hand tools—the people of the forests felled just a few, allowed their stumps to sprout, and then harvested this wood as a crop. The technique is called **coppicing**, and it was a vitally important part of life in the European forests for thousands of years. It was also carried to North

America—there are coppiced maples in Massachusetts that date back to the mid-18th century. Strangely, trees that are given this rather brutal treatment live much longer than trees that are left standing. European ash, for example, normally lives for about 200 years at most—but in England there are huge coppiced ash trees that were first cut more than 1,000 years ago, yet are still alive today.

Blown Away

Coppicing allowed the early Europeans to obtain all the timber they needed without destroying the forest. But in the temperate forests of China, it was a different story.

Much of the soil in China is of a type called **loess**, which is extremely fine-grained. It can be blown on the wind, and in parts of the Chinese central plain it lies in great drifts

Sustainable Forests

Sustainable use means harvesting natural products at the same or a lower rate than they need to replace themselves. In sustainable temperate forests, only a few trees are felled at a time. These trees are soon replaced by natural growth without the forest getting smaller overall. That way, any animals that are displaced are be able to find new homes within the forest easily. In addition, topsoil is less likely to get washed away by rain as is often the case when large areas of forests have been stripped. Sustainable forestry is common in the United States, such as in the Appalachian Hardwood Forest, which extends into 12 states in the east of the country. Oak, maple, walnut, and hickory are just some of the types of trees that are used sustainably in the forest.

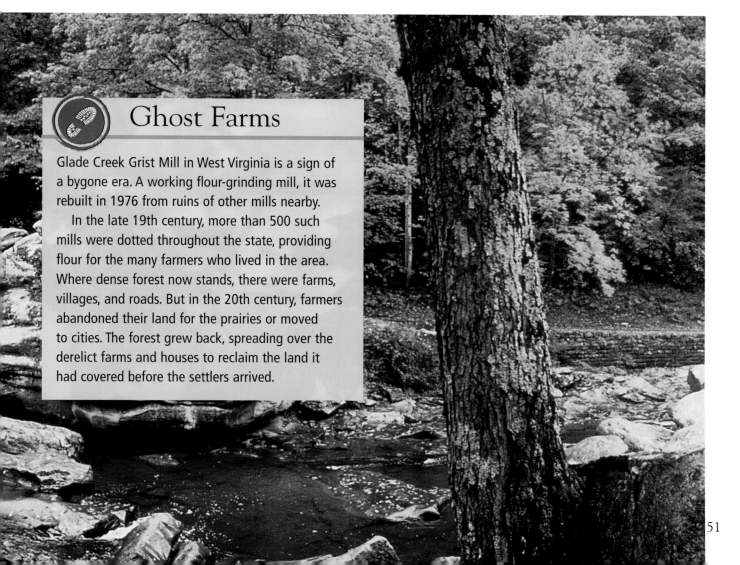

Ghost Farms

Glade Creek Grist Mill in West Virginia is a sign of a bygone era. A working flour-grinding mill, it was rebuilt in 1976 from ruins of other mills nearby.

In the late 19th century, more than 500 such mills were dotted throughout the state, providing flour for the many farmers who lived in the area. Where dense forest now stands, there were farms, villages, and roads. But in the 20th century, farmers abandoned their land for the prairies or moved to cities. The forest grew back, spreading over the derelict farms and houses to reclaim the land it had covered before the settlers arrived.

more than 60 meters (200 feet) deep. Loess is very fertile, and also makes good building material in the form of mud bricks. For the early Chinese farmers, it was very tempting to strip the trees away and turn the land into fields. They did exactly that, and by 4,000 years ago, the temperate forests that once covered lowland China had disappeared.

There was a catch, though. Without tree roots to hold it together, the loess could dry out and blow away, or be swept away in floods. This process, known as soil erosion, is now a big problem in China.

Getting rid of the forest also destroyed nearly all the native plants and animals. Today, rare Chinese animals like the giant panda live only in patches of mountain forest that are too steep and rugged to be turned into farmland. These forests rise like tree-clad islands from surrounding seas of fields, and the animals that live on each island are cut off from their neighbors. They are forced to

breed with close relatives, which can have harmful effects on their offspring. This process, called inbreeding, is a serious threat to the future of giant pandas.

Pandas also suffer from food shortages, because the bamboo they eat has a habit of flowering once every 40–60 years and then dying over large areas. The pandas must move on to find food, but since they cannot move off their islands, they starve. When the bamboo in the Wanglang Panda Reserve flowered and died in 1974, most of the 196 giant pandas in the reserve died, too. Since there are only about 1,400 giant pandas left on the planet, this was a catastrophe.

Destruction and Revival

Far to the southeast of China, New Zealand was once covered in unspoiled temperate rain forest. People first arrived about 1,000 years ago, sailing from islands in the Pacific. Today, their descendants are called the **Maoris**.

Return of the Forest

Temperate forest used to completely cover the state of Massachusetts in the eastern United States. But after the Pilgrims arrived in 1620, European settlers quickly began to cut the forest down and use the land for farming. Within 200 years, only small pockets of forest remained. Things changed again in the 19th century. New industries were developing in cities, and many people left their farms to seek their fortune. By the beginning of the 20th century, the forest had grown back over abandoned farms to cover 30 percent of the state. It continues spreading into the 21st century, and now covers about two-thirds of Massachusetts. The maps below show how forest grew back in a study site about 90 kilometers (55 miles) wide in northern Massachusetts between 1830 and 2005. Green represents forest and brown is open land.

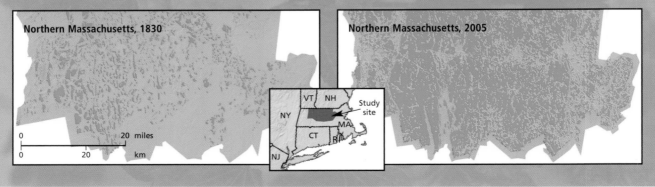

The Maoris' ancestors cleared the forest almost as soon as they arrived, mainly by burning. By the time the British captain James Cook (1728–1779) came to explore New Zealand in 1769, half the forest was gone.

Yet the Maoris do not seem to have used much of the land for farming. They probably set fire to the forest to smoke out giant flightless birds called moas. This hunting technique worked so well that much of the forest disappeared and moas became extinct.

The Maoris sailed to New Zealand from the Pacific islands of Polynesia, perhaps using boats like this traditional wooden canoe. Today such canoes are used only for races or festivals.

Total Loss

Although most of eastern China's forests were destroyed thousands of years ago, many large patches survived on hills until as recently as 1958. But then Chairman Mao Zedong announced the "Great Leap Forward," a project designed to drag rural China into the industrial age.

Villagers were ordered to start ironworks, using charcoal as fuel to melt the iron. Charcoal is made from wood, so the villagers had to cut down much of the surviving woodlands. They managed to make some iron, but the whole project was a failure, and the forests were destroyed for nothing.

In North America, the Native American tribes of the temperate forests had a far less destructive way of life. The economy of forest peoples like the Iroquois and Algonquian tribes was based on small-scale cultivation of corn, beans, and squash in forest clearings, as well as hunting and fishing. Their culture involved a reverence for nature that made large-scale forest clearance unthinkable. So when the *Mayflower* dropped anchor at Plymouth, Massachusetts, in late 1620, bringing the first English settlers to New England, the eastern forests were still intact.

The colonists started clearing the land for farms immediately. Within 200 years, most of New England was farmland, and only 30 percent was still forest. But, as the settlers pushed beyond the Appalachians, they found lands that were much easier to farm. The New England farmers began to pack up and head west, and by 1900, many of the fields that their ancestors had cleared were becoming forest again. Today, about 70 percent of New England is forest, although you can still find the ruins of old farmsteads and mills hidden among the trees.

A Valuable Resource

In Europe, people cleared vast areas of forest for farms in the early Middle Ages, but then they suddenly stopped. The interruption was caused by an epidemic called the Black Death, which wiped out a third of Europe's population between 1348 and 1350. By the time the population recovered, farming was becoming more efficient, so there was enough farmland to keep everyone fed.

The surviving forests became too valuable to be destroyed. They were vital to new industries that were developing in Europe, such as construction, ship-building, and ironworking. Iron was smelted in furnaces fueled by charcoal, and charcoal was made from coppiced wood. Similarly, most houses and ships were built from the timber of hardwood trees like oak. Since this was often in limited supply, it was conserved by foresters who made sure that felled trees were replaced by new saplings.

As long as they were economically valuable, the forests of Europe were fairly safe. But technology moves on. In the 19th century, coal replaced charcoal as the main furnace fuel, and hardwoods were no longer used for building. So ancient woodlands lost their value and started to disappear. In England, about 10 percent of the original temperate forest survived from 1350 to 1850, but half of this surviving forest has now vanished.

Virtual Wilderness

Many of the world's people now live and work in cities that were founded on the wealth created by the rich forest soils. The temperate forests—or rather the human landscapes that have replaced them—are the most densely populated of all biomes. But city life can be

This 14th-century picture shows a priest blessing plague victims. The Black Death—a massive outbreak of plague—killed one-third of Europe's population. After the outbreak, deforestation halted in Europe.

Camping trips are a good way to get a taste of the wilderness without sacrificing all our modern comforts.

stressful, and people now turn to the wilderness for relaxation—the forests have become part of the leisure industry.

Very little of the world's surviving temperate forest is truly wild. Most is managed, and much is secondary forest that regrew over abandoned farmland. Provided the trees are the native types that grew in the original wild forest, then native plants and animals can live among. Weekenders can wander into the forests, and get some idea of what they were like 10,000 years ago, before the invention of the ax.

Hot Stuff

To you it might be just barbecue fuel, but charcoal is amazing stuff. It's wood that has been half-burned in very little air to convert it into virtually pure carbon. If this is burned in a furnace with a good air supply, it produces a huge amount of heat—much more than the original wood. It is hot enough to melt metal, and when people realized this, maybe 5,000 years ago, it enabled them to start using copper, bronze, and eventually iron. So charcoal made from coppiced forest trees became vital to industry and civilization, right up until the 18th century.

SOUTHEAST AUSTRALIA

In the southeast corner of Australia, forests of eucalyptus trees flourish in the heavy rainfall. In the wettest places they form temperate rain forest, which stretches down to Tasmania.

Up a Gum Tree

Eucalyptus leaves are poisonous to most animals, but a few Australian animals have a digestive system that can deal with the poisons. The most famous is the koala. It has powerful jaws to grind the leaves to a fine pulp, and bacteria living in its digestive system convert the tough leaf fiber into sugar. When a baby koala is born it has no bacteria, so it cannot eat leaves. Its mother squirts some half-digested, bacteria-filled leaf pulp out of her back end, and her baby eats this to start its own bacteria colony! Koalas are becoming scarce. Loss of habitat and a disease called chlamydia are to blame.

Fact File

▲ Because of their unique wildlife, some Australian temperate forests are classed as UNESCO World Heritage Sites—places of outstanding natural importance to the common heritage of humanity.

▲ The Australian temperate rain forest provides a home for the world's tallest flowering plant: the 100-meter (330-foot) mountain ash.

▲ Eucalyptus trees are famed for the fragrant oil in their leaves. People use the oil in medication for coughs and colds.

▲ In February and March, 2009, wildfires raged across forests (right) and farmland in the state of Victoria, Australia. More than 170 people died in the fires.

1. Great Dividing Range
A chain of mountains runs along the east coast of Australia. Clouds sweeping in off the Pacific Ocean bring regular rain to the mountains. East of the range, urban and agricultural sprawl are removing the habitats of native animals.

2. Brisbane
This city lies near the northern limit of the temperate forest.

3. Border Group Reserves
Part of the Central Eastern Rainforest Reserves, these areas have the highest concentration of frog, snake, bird, and marsupial species in Australia.

4. Sydney
Australia's cultural center and largest city, with a population of almost 4 million. Urban sprawl is encroaching on the habitats of wildlife.

5. Murray River
This river runs west of the mountains, where the climate is drier and there is little forest.

6. Snowy River National Park
One of many wildlife preserves in the Great Dividing Range. The park is home to many threatened animals, including the spotted quoll and long-footed potoroo.

7. Mount Kosciusko
The highest point of the Great Dividing Range, this peak stands at 2,229 meters (7,311 feet).

8. Otway Ranges
An area of temperate rain forest with a high canopy of southern beeches covered with epiphytes. The ranges include the Great Otway National Park.

9. Mount Field National Park
The lush temperate rain forest, gorges, and peaks of this park are popular with walkers.

10. Tasmania Wilderness
This group of four national parks is a rare example of southern hemisphere temperate wilderness. Tasmanian devils are under threat from an infectious cancer spread during mating.

Below: Only about 5 percent of Tasmania's eucalyptus forest is protected. Much of this ancient forest has been logged. There are campaigns to protect more of the forest.

N

Cape York Peninsula

NORTH AMERICA   EUROPE   ASIA

AFRICA

SOUTH AMERICA

AUSTRALIA

ANTARCTICA

Coral Sea

Great Dividing Range

Great Barrier Reef

QUEENSLAND

AUSTRALIA

Darling Downs

Brisbane [2]

Sturt Desert

Great Artesian Basin

[1]

Great Dividing Range

[3]

Darling River

NEW SOUTH WALES

Lachlan River

[4] Sydney

Flinders Ranges

Murrumbidgee River

Murray River

[5]

Canberra

Snowy River National Park

CAPITAL TERRITORY

Adelaide

VICTORIA

[6]

[7]

Melbourne

Mount Bogong

Mount Kosciusko

Tasman Sea

Otway Ranges

[8]

Bass Strait

Flinders Island

King Island

Cape Barren Island

TASMANIA

Mount Ossa

Butlers Gorge   [9]   Mount Field National Park

Tasmania Wilderness   [10]

Hobart

Tasmania

0   300 miles

0   300 kilometers

THE FUTURE

The temperate forests are in the most densely populated parts of the world. If they are to survive, we have to manage them carefully.

The corks used to keep wine inside bottles are made from the thick bark of the cork oak tree, which grows in patches of temperate forest in the western Mediterranean. Every 10 years or so, farmers strip the bark from the cork oak trees, and the trees quickly grow a new layer.

In Spain and Portugal, cork oak forests have been harvested this way for centuries. They are not truly wild woodlands, but they are rich in wildlife, and harbor such animals as the Spanish imperial eagle, eagle owl, Iberian lynx, and wild boar.

Cork forests have been under threat in recent years. Many wine producers began to use plastic corks, which unlike real corks do not give wine a musty taste, and the demand for cork was reduced. Thousands of trees have been felled so that the land can be used for more profitable crops. However, there is hope. Portuguese scientists have recently found a way of chemically treating real corks so that they do not affect the flavor of wine.

These cork oaks in Spain are unharmed even though farmers have harvested a layer of bark from their trunk.

Although conservationists try to stop deforestation, the future of the cork forests is really down to economics. If there is a market for cork, these ancient forests will survive. If not, they will probably disappear.

Living Factories

Temperate forests all over the world face similar threats. Very little temperate forest is truly wild: most has been managed to produce regular crops of big timber trees or coppiced underwood. It might look like vandalism when trees are cut down, but it is often just part of the cropping process that keeps the forest in business. To people, forests are living factories that happen to provide homes for all sorts of wild plants and animals. If the factories go out of business, the wildlife has nowhere to go.

This happened in Great Britain when people abandoned firewood and charcoal in favor of coal and oil. Most of the timber used for firewood and charcoal came from coppiced woodland; when the market dried up, the foresters stopped coppicing the trees. The

trees grew bigger and the woodlands grew wilder, but they were making no money for the people who owned them. When the owners discovered that there was more money in destroying the woodlands and using the land for something else, that's what happened.

It is still happening, because the woodlands have no obvious economic value. The big timber trees are worth money, but they take so long to grow that many landowners prefer

These days, temperate forests—such as this one in North Carolina—are better understood for their animal and plant diversity and valued as places for leisure activities, such as hiking.

to fell them, sell them, and use the land for something else, such as building or farming.

Ancient native woodlands are often replaced by plantations of fast-growing softwoods—trees like pine and spruce—that

 ## Saving Pandas

One of the biggest problems facing the giant panda of China is isolation. Many pandas live in small patches of bamboo forest, cut off from each other. To overcome this problem, wildlife agencies are trying to link up the patches with thin strips of forest called corridors. This should encourage pandas to move about and interbreed, and should help them escape to different areas of forest if their local food supply fails.

Eventually, this method may be used to link several panda reserves into an enormous super-reserve. This will give the giant pandas a chance to live as they used to, before the farmers came and cut down most of their forest home.

Climate Change

A major threat to the temperate forests comes from climate change. When our power plants and cars use fossil fuels like coal and gasoline, they release carbon dioxide gas into the atmosphere. This is the main gas that causes the greenhouse effect, which happens when gases stop heat from escaping into space. High concentrations of carbon dioxide in the atmosphere are causing global warming.

This warming is upsetting the world's climates. In the North Atlantic, for example, melting arctic ice is disrupting the ocean currents that carry warm water north to Europe, so western Europe may get colder. Whether the climate gets warmer or colder, the forests will have to adapt to the change.

In the past, ice ages came and went, and the forests came and went with them. But this happened over thousands of years. The modern climate is changing much faster, and the trees may not be able to keep up. They could start dying out in the south because of drought, but not spread north fast enough to compensate. So the temperate forest in North America could dwindle to a tiny remnant in New England—along with all the forest wildlife.

Wild garlic flowers cover the ground in this part of the Bialowieza Forest, Poland. A national park since the 1920s, the forest is home to many wild mammals, including wolves, bison, boars, and lynx.

can be sold as a cash crop within a few years. A lot of Christmas trees are grown like this. These softwood trees often come from different countries, and the native animals don't like them. As a result, a whole wild community of animals and plants disappears.

The Bright Side

It's not all bad news. Many temperate forests are now protected as nature reserves. Some are still regularly cropped for timber, creating wonderful shifting communities of flowers that grow in the sunlit clearings. The reserve wardens keep cutting the timber to make sure the flowers survive, and they can sell the logs to help support the reserve.

Other forests, like those in the northern Appalachian Mountains, have become wilderness again, and they stand a good chance of staying that way. As the trees get older, the forests will grow wilder. The old trees rot and develop holes, providing homes for a greater variety of animals. Eventually the forests return to their primeval state.

Silent Forests

In the past, temperate forests were always made up of native trees—plants that had lived in the region for thousands of years. But since people started importing seeds and plants from other countries, more and more foreign, or exotic, trees began to grow in the forests.

Local insects often cannot live on these exotic trees. This creates a barrier in the food chain, reducing food for local insect-eating birds and animals. In a few cases, native animals do adapt to the introduced trees. However, many newly planted forests will never support the rich variety of life found in the old native woodlands.

Meanwhile, there are still a few patches of truly wild, unspoiled temperate forest, such as the great Bialowieza Forest in eastern Poland. They have never been felled or managed, and probably never will be. With luck, these survivals from the distant past will endure long into the future.

Saving the Planet

One way of tackling global warming is to plant more trees, like this horse chestnut seedling. As trees grow, they absorb carbon dioxide from the air and lock it up for hundreds of years. Since woodlands also make wonderful wildlife reserves and leisure attractions, reforestation projects are becoming more and more common across the world. There may never be enough to stop global warming, but they certainly help save the planet.

61

GLOSSARY

acid rain: Rain in which the water has reacted with pollutants in the atmosphere to form acids. Acid rain is harmful to plants and animals.

atmosphere: The layer of air around Earth.

biome: A major division of the living world, distinguished by its climate and wildlife. Tundra and desert are examples of biomes.

bulb: A kind of fattened root used by a plant for storage of food.

carbon dioxide: A gas released when fuel burns. Carbon dioxide is one of the main gases causing global warming.

chlorophyll: A green chemical in the leaves and stems of plants that captures the energy in sunlight and helps convert it to food.

climate: The pattern of weather that happens in one place during an average year.

cold-blooded: Having a body temperature that depends on the surroundings. Reptiles are cold-blooded, for example.

conifer: A type of plant that does not have true fruit like flowering plants, but instead produces seeds protected inside a cone. Conifers often have needle-shaped leaves.

coppice: A woodland that people manage, to produce timber growing from the base of living trees.

deciduous: A plant that sheds its leaves every year.

desert: A biome that receives less than 250 millimeters (10 inches) of rain a year.

domestic animals: Animals kept by people, such as pets and livestock.

dormant: So inactive as to appear lifeless. Plant seeds often stay dormant until their soil gets wet.

equator: An imaginary line around Earth, midway between the poles.

evaporate: To turn into gas. When water evaporates, it becomes an invisible part of the air.

evergeen: A plant that keeps its leaves all year round.

fertile: Soil that is capable of sustaining plant growth is termed fertile. Farmers try to make soil more fertile when growing crops.

fungus: A type of organism, neither plant nor animal, that gets its food by digesting plant or animal material, living or dead.

geyser: A jet of hot water or steam produced by volcanic activity.

global warming: The gradual warming of Earth's climate, caused by pollution of the atmosphere.

hemisphere: One half of Earth. The northern hemisphere is the half to the north of the equator.

herbaceous plant: A plant that has no woody tissue. Many herbaceous plants die back in winter.

hibernation: A time of dormancy that some animals go through during winter. In true hibernation, the heart rate and breathing slow dramatically and the body cools.

ice age: A period when Earth's climate was cooler and the polar ice caps expanded. The last ice age ended 10,000 years ago.

loess: A wind-blown dust that forms soft soils.

Maori: A people now living in New Zealand. They first arrived there 1,000 or more years ago.

metabolism: An animal's or plant's chemical process of breaking down food to release energy.

microclimate: The pattern of weather within a small area, such as a valley, treetop, or burrow.

migration: A long-distance journey by an animal to find a new home. Many animals migrate each year.

nomad: A person who travels from place to place in search of food and water, instead of settling permanently.

nutrient: Any chemical in the soil that plants need.

perennial: A plant that lives for several or many years.

podocarp: A type of conifer that grows in the temperate rain forest in the southern hemisphere.

pollination: The transfer of pollen from the male part of a flower to the female part of the same flower or another flower, causing the flower to produce seeds.

prairie: A large area of grassland in central North America.

predator: An animal that catches and eats other animals.

protein: One of the major food groups. It is used for building and repairing plant and animal bodies.

rain forest: A lush forest that receives frequent heavy rainfall. Tropical rain forests grow in the tropics; temperate rain forests grow in cooler places.

rain shadow: An area where rainfall is low because nearby mountains obstruct rain-bearing winds.

sap: The body liquid of plants.

shrubland: A biome that mainly contains shrubs, such as the chaparral of California.

skink: A type of lizard, usually with very smooth scales.

species: A particular type of organism. Cheetahs are a species, for instance, but birds are not, because there are lots of different bird species.

Stone Age: A period in human prehistory when people used stone tools but had not yet invented metal tools.

subtropical: A region of Earth within the temperate zone, but near, and similar to, the tropics. Florida is often called subtropical.

taiga: A biome in northern regions that mainly contains conifer trees.

temperate: Between the warm tropics and the cold, polar regions.

temperate forest: A biome of the temperate zone that mainly contains broadleaf trees.

temperate grassland: A biome of the temperate zone that mainly contains grassland.

tropic of Cancer: An imaginary line around Earth about 2,600 kilometers (1,600 miles) north of the equator.

tropic of Capricorn: An imaginary line around Earth about 2,600 kilometers (1,600 miles) south of the equator.

tropical: Between the tropics of Cancer and Capricorn. Tropical countries are warm all year.

tropical forest: Forest in Earth's tropical zone, such as tropical rain forest or monsoon forest.

tropical grassland: A tropical biome in which grass is the main form of plant life.

tundra: A biome of the far north, made up of treeless plains covered with small plants.

vapor: A gas formed when a liquid evaporates.

warm-blooded: Having a warm body temperature constantly. Mammals are warm-blooded.

Further Research

Books

Allaby, Michael. *Temperate Forests*. New York: Facts on File, 2007.
Kuennecke, Bernd H. *Temperate Forest Biomes*. Westport, CT: Greenwood Press, 2008.
Wojahn, Rebecca A. and Donald Wojahn. A *Temperate Forest Food Chain*. Minneapolis, MN: Lerner Classroom, 2008.

Websites

ParkNet: www.nps.gov/grsm
(Links to official national park websites)
Glossopedia: www.globio.org/glossopedia/article.aspx?art_id=3
(Useful facts about temperate forests.)
The Forest Biome: www.ucmp.berkeley.edu/exhibits/biomes/forests.php
(In-depth descriptions of types of forests.)

INDEX

Picture Credits

Key: l – left, r – right, m – middle, t – top, b – bottom.

Front Cover: Shutterstock: Igumnova Irina.
Ardea: Liz and Tony Bomforf 23; David Dixon 19; Thomas Dressler 58; Jean-Paul Ferrero 17; A. Greensmith 6r, 29; Don Hadden 32 (inset); John Mason 31; Steffan Mayers 36; Jaime Plaza Van Roon 11; J. E. Swedberg 26; **Art Explosion:** 43t, 45t; **Bruce Coleman:** Jane Burton 35 (inset); Mr. P. Clement 35t/r; Gerald S. Cubitt 32; P. Kaya 61; Joe McDonald 38; Orion Press 7m/l, 46; Hans Reinhard 24t; Kim Taylor 34, 45b; Staffan Widstrand 49; **Corbis:** Adrian Arbib 60; Tony Arruza 59; Bettmann Archive 51; Frank Lane Picture Agency 43b; Steve Kaufmann 47; George McCarthy 40b; Joe McDonald 40t; Douglas Peebles 22; Robert Pickett 18; Neil Rabinowitz 53; Science Pictures Limited 41b; Karen Su 44b; **Digital Stock:** World Panoramas 7m/r, 7r, 12/13; **Image Bank:** Macduff Everton 50; Terry Donnelly 14; Pete Turner 28; **istockphoto:** 56b, 57; **NASA:** Planetary Photojournal 48; **NHPA:** A.N.T. Photo Library 44t, 56t; Laurie Campbell 24b, 30b/r; Manfred Danegger 42; John Shaw 9, 21; **PhotoDisc:** Don Farrall 39; Robert Glusic 4m; Jack Hollingsworth 5m; Russell Illig 8, 30l; Photolink 1, 5r, 6m, 7l, 14 (inset), 15, 26t/l, 27b/r, 41t; Karl Weatherly 4r; **Pictor International:** 55; Public Domain: 32(inset), 54b; John Gerald Keulemans/G.D Rowley's Ornithological Miscellany 37; **Shutterstock:** Nicole Kessel 41t;

The Brown Reference Group Ltd. has made every attempt to contact the copyright holder. If anyone has any information please contact info@brownreference.com